T0209319

# *I Am Listening*

## *As Heard By Kathleen Santora*

## KATHLEEN SANTORA

**BALBOA**.PRESS
A DIVISION OF HAY HOUSE

Balboa Press books may be ordered through booksellers or by contacting:

Balboa Press
A Division of Hay House
1663 Liberty Drive
Bloomington, IN 47403
www.balboapress.com
1 (877) 407-4847

.Because of the dynamic nature of the Internet, any web addresses or links contained in this book may have changed since publication and may no longer be valid. The views expressed in this work are solely those of the author and do not necessarily reflect the views of the publisher, and the publisher hereby disclaims any responsibility for them.

The author of this book does not dispense medical advice or prescribe the use of any technique as a form of treatment for physical, emotional, or medical problems without the advice of a physician, either directly or indirectly. The intent of the author is only to offer information of a general nature to help you in your quest for emotional and spiritual well-being. In the event you use any of the information in this book for yourself, which is your constitutional right, the author and the publisher assume no responsibility for your actions.

Any people depicted in stock imagery provided by Getty Images are models, and such images are being used for illustrative purposes only. Certain stock imagery © Getty Images.

Print information available on the last page.

ISBN: 978-1-9822-5002-7 (sc)
ISBN: 978-1-9822-5003-4 (e)

Balboa Press rev. date: 06/24/2020

# Run to You

I just want to run to you
I only want to hear your voice
Only want to feel your love
Telling me this all a dream
Telling me look for the light and see
Total love within me You can never leave my side
There is nothing in this world
Making my love for you die
Reveal all your thoughts to me
So i can set you free
A new world that lives within
Without sorrow or sin
I just want to run to you
You tell me we are all here to save the world
We to hold each others hand and stand for love
I just want to run to you
Forgetting all the things i thought i knew
Seeing a new way with you
Being part of the universe
That stands for love above all else
Being in my safety place
Being who i really am
Loves child of light
With a brand new sight
I just want to run to you
Filling up my heart with love
So i can rise above
All the chaos and stress
Being part of gods quest for love
Spreading over the earth

Making things right
So we call all lives to the light
I just want to run to you
Because the things we do
We do in the light of you
Receiving all this
When i run to you
Singing all my praise to you

# This Moment

I JUST WANT TO STAY….IN THIS MOMENT
THIS MOMENT…THAT I BELIEVE
THIS MOMENT THAT GIVES ME SO MUCH JOY
THIS MOMENT…IM LETTING YOUR LOVE IN
THIS MOMENT… I HAVE SO MUCH FAITH
THIS MOMENT THAT… I BELIEVE
I JUST WANT TO STAY…IN THIS MOMENT
LETTING YOUR VOICE SOOTH MY TIRED SOUL
LETTING YOUR VOICE LEADING TO THE PATH OF
HOME
STAYING ING THIS MOMENT OF LOVE
FEELING ALL THE LIGHT
I JUST WANT TO STAY… IN THIS MOMENT
NEEDING NOTHING ELSE
I JUST WANT TO STAY… IN THIS MOMENT
FEELING FREE AND NOTHING ELSE
I JUST WANT TO STAY…IN THIS MOMENT
LETTING ALL MY TROUBLES GO
KNOWING YOU WALK THIS WALK WITH ME
SHOWING ME THE WAY
I JUST WANT TO STAY…IN THIS MOMENT
FEELING THE RAPTURE OF YOUR LOVE SWIRLING IN
MY SOUL
KNOW THAT THE UNIVERSE LOVES ME
BEING HOME KNOWING YOU ARE NEAR
I JUST WANT TO STAY…IN THIS MOMENT
LETTING IN THE LIGHT
LETTING ALL MY TROUBLES GO

*Kathleen Santora*

LETTING IN THE LIGHT
I JUST WANT TO STAY …IN THIS MOMENT
LETTING TIME STAND STILL
LETTING ALL THE JOY AND LOVE
THIS PRECIOUS MOMENT HAS TO GIVE

YOU HOLD MY SOUL
IN A PLACE SOMEHOW I KNOW
KEEPING SAFE MY SPIRIT WITH YOU
THERE IS NOTHING I CAN DO
TO BREAK THE BOND OF LIGHT INTO
THE WORLD OF LIGHT
THAT IS PROMISED TO
THE WORLD OF LIGHT AMONGST THE STARS
WHERE MY FATHER WAITS FOR ME
ALL I NEED TO DO IS SEE
WHAT WAITS FOR ME
MAY I HEAR THE VOICE THAT LEADS
FAR ABOVE THE TREES
PAST THE CLOUDS AND STARS OF NIGHT
THE PLACE THAT WAITS FOR ME
IN A PLACE I'LL CALL MY HOME
FOREVER MORE IN JUST MY SOUL
SEEING ONLY LIGHT AND GOOD WITHIN YOUR ARMS
IS IT ENOUGH TO SEE ME THROUGH
TO KNOW SOMEDAY I WILL COME TO YOU
RESTING FOREVER WHEN I DO
IN YOUR LOVE

# Flip - Flop (Rap)

Don't _____ flip- flop
Go to the side of love
Don't _____ flip flop
Don't go to the side of anger

Don't flip flop
Stand with the light be hind you
Don't flip flop

Go with the big guns of light
on't go with the little guns of death
Go where the real boys protect you
Not where the bad boys will kill you
Go with the bright lights of heaven
Not on a stage of darkness
But they'll put you on the stage of all of the Universe
Making you a star of all eternity So your blinking and shining and reaching out to all humanity
The right way not screaming and shouting and killing the earths way

Dont flip flop
Stay on the side of the Universe

# Innocence

Being in the innocence
Standing in the light
Is being all you're meant to be
Going up in flight
Being in the innocence
Of you meeting homes calling
Making love your plight
Being in the innocence
Let your mind be free
Standing in the light of love
Letting your spirit be free
Being in the innocence
Unleashing your heart
Sharing with the world our love
Knowing we are all a part
Being in each others light
Takes us to the place within
Where we al exist as one
One mind one heart
When we make the choice for good
We will see the world as a whole
Being in each others light
Being only one

# Need A Little Spirit

JUST NEED A LITTLE SPIRIT IN YOUR SOUL
WHEN YOU THINK YOUR BODY GETS WEAK
THAT'S WHEN YOU NEED TO SPEAK
WORDS OF LOVE
FROM HIGH ABOVE
JUST NEED A LITTLE SPIRIT IN YOUR SOUL
CHILD OF LIGHT
FULL OF MIGHT
WORDS TO HEAL
SO YOU CAN FEEL
JUST NEED A LITTLE SPIRIT IN YOUR SOUL
LET YOUR LIGHT SHINE BRIGHT
ITS A BEAUTIFUL SIGHT
WHEN YOUR LIGHT SHINES BRIGHT
JUST NEED A LITTLE SPIRIT IN YOUR SOUL
CREATING WONDERFUL LIGHT
BEING FULL OF JOY
SENDING LOVE FOR ALL
JUST NEED A LITTLE BIT OF SPIRIT IN YOUR SOUL
WHEN YOUR DOWN AND OUT
AND FULL OF DARKNESS
JUST NEED A LITTLE SPIRIT IN YOUR SOUL
YOU NEED TO RAISE YOUR EYES TO THE SPIRIT ON HIGH
JUST NEED A LITTLE SPIRIT IN YOUR SOUL

# This is A Holy Thing

MY SPIRIT IS A HOLY THING
WHEN I GET UP AND SING
WHEN I CLOSE MY EYES
I SEE LIGHT INSIDE
WHEN I OPEN MY HEART, LOVE COMES OUT

CHORUS
IT IS A HOLY THING
WHEN I SING HIS PRAISE, MY SPIRIT GETS RAISED
WHEN I HERE YOUR WORDS, LIFTS ME UP TO SERVE

CHORUS
LIFT UP MY ARMS IN PRAISE,
LIFT MY VOICE AND SING
THIS IS A HOLY THING (LOUDER WITH MORE BOUNCE)
MY SPIRIT LOVES TO SING
MY SPIRIT LOVES TO SING
IT NEEDS LOVE AND JOY
IT NEEDS A SONG TO BE FREE
LET MY VOICE RING OUT
LET MY SPIRIT OUT
THIS IS A HOLY THING (LOUDER)
WHEN YOU ARE HERE WITH ME
I KNOW THAT I AM FREE
NO MORE WANDERING (This is a Holy Thing 1ST SECTION)
NO MORE SEARCHING (2ND SECTION)
ONLY FEELING FREE (3RD SECTION)
THIS IS A HOLY THING (EVERYONE AND LOUDER)
MAKE ME SCREAM AND SHOUT
CAUSE I HAVE NO DOUBT

*Kathleen Santora*

THIS IS A HOLY THING
THIS IS A HOLY THING
HELP ME LIGHT THE WORLD
WITH THE SONG FROM ABOVE
SENDING LIGHT THROUGHOUT
THIS IS A HOLY THING THIS IS A HOLY THING THIS IS
A HOLY THING

# Singing Angels

HIGH ABOVE THE CLOUDS AT NIGHT
YOU CAN HEAR THE ANGELS IN FLIGHT
AS THE STARS ARE SHINING BRIGHT
FLOATING ABOVE TO GIVE US LIGHT
THIER LOVE IS REACHING DOWN
SENDING PROTECTION ALL AROUND
SINGING ANGELS UP ABOVE
GIVING COMFORT TOUCHING US WITH LOVE
OPEN YOUR HEART HEAR THIER SONG
SO WE KNOW WE'RE NOT ALONE
LETTING US KNOW ARE SOULS ARE PRECIOUS
SAFE WITHIN THE SIGHT OF GODS BLESSINGS
THEY KEEP THEM SAFE WITHIN HEAVEN
UNTIL WE ARE READY TO CLAIM THEM
HIGH ABOVE THE CLOUDS AT NIGHT
YOU CAN HEAR THE ANGELS IN FLIGHT
BE STILL AND LET LOVE IN
KNOW THAT THIER PRESENCE IS NEAR
KNOW THAT THEY ARE WITH YOU AND ALWAYS NEAR
HIGH ABOVE THE CLOUDS AT NIGHT

# Inspiration

send me inspiration for my life
give me power inside tonight
i need purpose while I'm here
keep it real and send me truth
send me what you would have me do
send me inspiration for my life
take me down the road once more
bring me to the open door
of love of love so i can sing songs of love forever more send me
inspiration for my life
fill my eyes with love and light
seeing purpose in all of this
so i know why i came to this place
send me inspiration for my life
have no time to wait right now
i just need to be shown somehow
just for love
just for love
now I'm here and shining shining
filled with inspiration like lightning
doing what is kind and good
doing what every soul should do taking me to that higher place
so i can live forever in peace
i need inspiration in my life

# Walk These Halls of Darkness

## (ballad)

As I walk these halls of darkness
Searching for the light
I ask my soul and God alone
Why do you have me here

A place where I feel lost
And do not belong
Trying to do your work
Trying to live your word

Sometimes I don't understand
Why am I Here
And then I hear
IIIIIIIII am preparing you for so
Much Love

I hear his voice
Teaching me patience
I hear his voice
Teaching me to look past all sadness

I hear his voice
Teaching me no judgement
I hear his voice saying
IIIIIII am preparing you for so much love

I begin to see innocence
I begin to see light in all things
I begin to know in my mind
That my path is planned

He is preparing me to do his good works
He is preparing me with so much strength
He has showed me darkness to light
And I hear him say
I am preparing you for so much love

# The Light Has Come (Sung in A Soft Whisper of Joy)

The light has come
Don't want to waste another minute
Want to look and see what's in it

The light has come
Need to see what they want to show me
Need to get the love they want to give me

The light has come
My soul is shining brighter
Connected to the ray of light I'm higher
The light has come

Look at me and how it changed my aura
Look at me when I'm at my purest
The light has come

I am free
No one needs to tell me
Because now I see
When it came I felt the change
My heart opened wide
My soul took over
I felt peace in every space within me
When the light rushed over me

I know now how it feels
No one needs to shoe me
I just go within
Feeling it always within me
The light has come

This is what we wait for
I always knew it would find me
The darkness is gone
I carry the light with me
No matter where I go
No matter what life brings me
The light has come

No one needs to bring it to me
The light has come
I know where I belong
The light has come
I belong to love
In a whisper it was here
In a blink I feel the change
Giving me hope and strength to walk to his earth
Knowing I belong to the light
Carrying it with me all my life
The light has come

# Bleeding Hearts

Bleeding Heart
Sadness and shame
Bleeding hearts
No one to blame
Keeping their pain inside
Breaking their own hearts
Following the darkness
Of their own thoughts
Angles cry with you
They want you to heal
Grieving for your soul
Because they want you to know
There is so much love for you, there is so much love for you
They see only your light
They see deep inside you
Where you are only bright
Bleeding heart
You are love unconditionally
The Universe has love
There are no conditions
Bleeding hearts
Give them over to heal
The Universe is here
The path they will show you
It is all very real Just look for the light
And you will see it before you
Bleeding hearts know you are loved
You are only sleeping
The Angels will walk with you
Until you awake
And your heart stops bleeding and your soul will mend

# Restoration (Choir)

Is is a Restoration of love
Of Love
Brought down form the heavens above
Above
Sent with a flash of light
Of light, of light Into the hearts of man
To lift our energy
To let love be revealed
It is a Restoration of love
Brought down from the Heavens above
Here to spread from heart to heart
To teach we are not apart
To say our minds are one
To show us as one, the way to home
To feel each others light
So as a whole we shine bright
It is a restoration of love
Brought from the Heavens above
Hearing only the voice, that guides our Sprit inside
It is a Restoration of love
Brought from the Heavens above
Stand within that light
Feel the power and might
It is a Restoration of love
It is a restoration of love
Turning our minds to good
Nothing else need to exists
Only love, only love
It is a restoration of love
Take the hand of light, take the hand of light

It is a restoration of love
It makes everything right
It is a restoration of love
It is a gift from the heavens
for those who's home is in heaven
It is a restoration of love
It is a restoration of love
It is restoration of love

# What If

What if
I didn't have the light to find me
What if
I didn't have the heavens to guide me
What if
I wasn't destined for grace to be in me
What if
I spent my whole life wondering

If I couldn't reach for his hand
And If I didn't hear him call me name
What would I be, but a lonely soul

What if
With no place to go
No way to right my wrongs
No way to mend my heart

What if
Life having no meaning
Sight not really seeing
Running on the path to home
Knowing, knowing that is where I belong
Because I know, What it

# Angels Watching

the angels are watching they are looking down on us
looking down from the heavens
telling us "you are one of us"
telling us to dig deep inside
to where you really exist
deep within your soul
way beyond what this is
we can all find total love
everyone has it inside
total love is what you really are
just reach deep inside
we can change the earth by just our
thoughts
they are stronger then we think
all of us together
thinking of how to spare the earth
all of us thinking together using our power
within
hearing our souls speak to us
letting that energy go first
bringing the highest place within us
to save the earth
meet yourself at your own doorway
the altar to your soul
close your eyes and tell yourself
love is in control
stop fighting what you are not
the earth is not your home
we are only here to correct the earth
but your real home exists surrounded in total love

# A Song of Love

THIS IS A SONG OF LOVE
FOR YOU TO KEEP
THIS IS A SONG OF LOVE
MADE DEEP WITHIN THE ARMS OF PEACE
THIS IS A SONG OF LOVE
IN BELONGS IN YOUR HEART
SENT STRAIGHT FROM ANGELS
BORN IN THEIR WINGS
SENT DOWN TO BE RECEIVED
WITHIN YOUR SOUL
THE WAY IS ONLY LOVE
THAT IS THE ONLY PATH
TO FEEL THEM COME TO YOU
AMONGST THE VAST AND GLORIOUS PLACE
WHERE ONLY LOVE EXITS
HEAVEN IS THE PLACE
THEY SEND SONGS OF LOVE FOR YOU TO KEEP
THEY WHISPER GENTLE MELODIES IN YOUR SLEEP
THE SONGS CARRY THEIR LOVE
SO WHEN WE WAKE
WE BRING THE LOVE
FROM HIGH ABOVE
LISTEN—WITHIN
AND NOW THAT YOU KNOW
LISTEN—WITHIN
TO THE SONG OF LOVE

# Sweet Charity

sweet sweet sweet charity
rocking my soul with clarity
sweet sweet sweet charity
bathing my heart in happiness
sweet sweet sweet charity
bring me home where i belong
sweet sweet sweet charity
writing a song of love within me
all of us sharing love
rocking the love around the world
sweet sweet sweet charity
bringing love into the earth plane
with our rocking love we share
changing the earths atmosphere
making here a safer place of love
sweet sweet sweet charity
bringing us close to him rocking our love with him
sweet sweet charity

# I Will Gift You with Love

Bring me your sadness and pain Bring to me your sorrow
Come to me with an open heart and I will show you
Sit in my arms and I will gift you with love
Sit in my arms, be never lonely
Wake in a new day, make your life holy

(CHORUS)
Annnnnnd I..........will gift you with love
Whats there to give up, only anguish
Just bring your heart home never leaving

(CHORUS)
Annnnnnnd I......... will gift you with love Your soul holds the meaning of me
This is where you belong, always with me
Annnnnnd I......... will gift you with love

*I Am Listening*

## Whenever You Sleep

### (THIS IS A ROCK AND ROLL SOUND)


BACKGROUND LOUD SHOUTING

CHRIST SHOUTING SHOUTING FROM THE HEAVENS

REPEAT
WHENEVER YOU SLEEP
I AM WATCHING
WHENEVER YOU WAKE
I WALK WITH YOU
KEEP ME IN YOUR MIND
I'LL KEEP YOU IN MY ARMS
BREATHE IN MY LIGHT
SEE HOW LIFE CHANGES
HOLD MY HAND IN THE DARK
I'LL NEVER LEAVE YOU

BACKGROUND

WHAT COMES FROM GOODNESS
WHAT COMES FROM CHARITY
A NEW WAY TO SEE
WHEN YOU SEE THROUGH ME
REMEMBER MY WORDS
HOLDING MY HAND
YOU WILL NOT FALTER
HOLDING MY HAND
AS WE WALK TOGETHER

BACKGROUND

I NEED YOUR LOVE
TO LIVE IN THIS WORLD
I AM STILL HERE
THROUGH OUR LOVE

CHORUS
SEND OUT MY LOVE
SEND OUT MY LIGHT
SEND OUT MY WORDS
SEND IT NEAR SEND IT FAR

I AM HERE

# Send Me an Army of Angels

SEND ME AN ARMY OF ANGELS
SEND ME AN ARMY OF ANGELS
I HAVE NO DOUBT
THER'RE IN THE HOUSE
TO FIGHT THE FIGHT
WITH ALL THEY'RE MIGHT
SEND ME AN ARMY OF ANGELS
SEND ME AN ARMY OF ANGELS
WITH ALL THEY'RE LIGHT
BRING DOWN THE HOUSE
HEROS OF LOVE
FROM HIGH ABOVE
SEND ME AN ARMY OF ANGELS
SEND ME AN ARMY OF ANGLES
TO MAKE US STRONG
TO SERVE THE LORD
FIGHTING WITH LOVE
PREPARING THE WORLD
FOR WHEN HE'S HERE
SEND ME AN ARMY OF ANGELS
SEND ME AN ARMY OF ANGLES

REPEAT

# I Feel A Rumbling

I FEEL A RUMBLING
DEEP INSIDE
GOTTA LET IT OUT
RIGHT NOW
I FEEL A RUMBLING
I THINK ITS MY SOUL
READY TO SHARE THE JOY
DEEP WITHIN
THE HOLY SPIRITS HERE
HES CALLING MY NAME
HE MAKES ME WANT TO SING A SONG
IN HIS PRAISE
JUMP...WITH JOY
SING ...WITH JOY
PEAK...THE WORDS OF ANGELS
MAKE SOME NOISE
FOR THE LORD
RAISE YOUR VOICE
FOR THE LORD
I FEEL A RUMBLING
DEEP INSIDE
I FEEL A RUMBLING
MAKES ME WANNA CRY
CAUSE I FEEL YOUR LOVE
DEEP INSIDE
WE ARE A POWERHOUSE OF LOVE
WHEN WE ARE ALL TOGETHER
WE ARE A POWERHOUSE OF LOVE

WHEN WE BRING HIS PRAISE TOGETHER
WE ARE A POWERHOUSE OF LOVE
WHEN WE REACH OUR VOICES TO THE SKY
WE ARE A POWERHOUSE OF LOVE
I FEEL A RUMBLING INSIDE
REPEAT RAISING ENERGY

# To Be Found

DO YOU SEE WHAT IT MEANS
TO BE FOUND
DO YOU KNOW HOW IT FEELS
TO BE LOVED
WHAT NEEDS TO BE SAID
I BELIEVE

WHAT NEEDS TO BE DONE
WHAT HE TELLS ME
LIVING IN HIS WILL
LIVING IN HIS LIGHT
TAKING STEPS TOWARDS HOME
FOLLOWING HIS LIGHT

I MADE THE CHOICE
NOW I WILL LIVE IT
HAVE FAITH IN YOUR HEART
NEVER GIVE IN
IF YOUR SEARCH WITHIN YOUR HEART
HE WILL BE THERE

YOU HAVE THE STRENGTH
OF THE UNIVERSE
IN YOUR HANDS

# Help Me (Gospel)

HELP ME
HELP ME
HELP ME LORD
HELP ME
HELP ME
HELP ME LORD
HELP ME TO HEAR YOUR VOICE O LORD
HELP HELP ME
HELP ME LORD
HELP ME TO FIND YOUR LOVE
HELP ME
HELP ME
HELP ME LORD
GET ME TO THE MOUNTAIN TOP
HELP ME
HELP ME
HELP ME LORD
GIVE ME STRENGTH TO WALK TO YOU
HELP ME
HELP ME HELP ME HELP ME LORD
I WOKE UP AND FOUND YOU THERE
HELP ME
HELP ME
HELP ME LORD
NOW I'M FILLED WITH LOVE AND LIGHT
AND I'LL NEVER NEVER LEAVE YOUR SIDE

# So Far From Home

(CHORUS)
SO FAR FROM HOME
SO FAR FROM HOME
WE'RE SO FAR FROM HOME
ENLIGHTENED BEINGS WITHOUT A HOME
LOOKING EVERY WHICH WAY AND THAT
LOOKING FOR A PLACE THAT'S RIGHT

(CHORUS)
HERE WALKING AMONG THE CHAOS
PEOPLE FIGHTING AND LIVES LOST
KNOWING THIS ISN'T WHERE WE BELONG
LOOKING, LOOKING FOR OUR HOME

(CHORUS)
HERE WE ARE ENLIGHTENED BEING
STUCK IN A PLACE WHERE NOTHINGS JIVING
ENLIGHTENED BEINGS
LOOKING AT VIOLENCE
LOOKING AT MURDER

(CHORUS)
WE ARE POWERFUL BEINGS
USING IT FOR NONSENSE
TRYING TO STAY ABOVE THE NONSENSE WE ARE
SUPPOSED TO BE FLYING
THROUGH THE UNIVERSE
AMONG THE ANGELS

SEEING GOODNESS AND LIGHT
SEEING EACH OTHER AS BRIGHT STARS
NOT AS ENEMIES TRYING TO KILL EACH OTHER

(CHORUS)
SO LETS REMEMBER THAT
KNOWING IT ONLY TAKES OUR MIND
TO CHANGE THINGS
AND MAKE THIS A BETTER PLACE
TO BE IN
EVERYBODY'S GETTING HIGH
CAUSE THEY WANT TO GO THERE
EVERYBODY'S ACTING MAD
CAUSE THEY KNOW THEY DON'T BELONG HERE
BUT SOMEWHERE IN YOU..YOU KNOW …CAN I FLY
WITH YOU (SPOKEN NOT SUNG)

# Confines of Your Love

I WILL STAY
I WILL STAND
I WILL STAY WITHIN THE CONFINES OF YOUR LOVE
I WILL LIVE WITHIN THE LIFE THAT IS YET TO COME
I WILL BE WITH THE ANGELS FROM ABOVE
NEEDING ONLY YOUR LOVE
I WILL WALK BENEATH THE HEAVENS FROM ABOVE
KNOWING THEY ARE THERE FOR ME WITH LOVE
SEEING LIGHT IN EVERYTHING I DO
KNOW THAT I DO IT ALL FOR YOU
LET ME HOLD YOU ANGELS WITHIN MY HEART
SHOWING ME A LIFE THAT'S BEGINNING TO START
REALIZING ALL I NEED IS YOUR LOVE
IF I DIDN'T HAVE THE LIGHT WHAT WOULD I DO MY
SPIRIT SAYS COME TO ME NOW
MY HEART IS OPEN SHOW ME HOW
DEEP WITHIN MY SOUL I KNOW NOW
I JUST NEED THE LIGHT TO OPEN THE PATHWAYS OF
MY MIND
KNOWING WHAT I LOOK FOR I WILL FIND
BEING LOVED AND ONLY NEEDING THAT
HOLDING ME WITHIN THE CONFINES OF YOUR LOVE
I KNOW THAT THIS IS WHERE I BELONG
DEEP WITHIN THE PLACE I CALL MY SOUL
I AM HERE BUT NOT A PRISONER OF A BODY
MY SPIRIT IS FREE
WE ARE ALL FALLEN ANGELS LOOKING FOR OUR WAY
HOME
THE ONLY WAY TO GET THERE IS THROUGH LOVE

WHEN I WAKE I WILL BE WITHIN YOUR ARMS ONCE
AGAIN
IN MY REAL HOME AND THIS LIFE WILL BE JUST A
DREAM
RETURNING FOREVER TO THE CONFINES OF YOUR
LOVE
I WILL STAY

# Can I Sit With You A While

CAN I SIT WITH YOU A WHILE
CAN I REST IN YOUR ARMS
CAN I BE HOME IN THE SAFETY OF LOVE
FEELING UNIVERSAL LOVE
WE ALL GET WEARY
WE ALL GET TIRED
AND OUR WALK SEEMS LONG
WHEN WE SEE THROUGH THE EYES OF LIGHT
WHEN PURPOSE COMES AND CHANGES LIFE
WHEN WE KNOW WE ARE NEVER ALONE
ALWAYS LOOKING IN OUR MINDS
WE ALL HAVE THE NEED TO KNOW WHY
THE NEED TO LOOK FOR HOME
THE GRACE TO LOOK WITHIN
WILL BRING US THERE
WE ALL NEED PRAYER
AND THE WILLINGNESS TO HEAR THE ANSWERS FROM
ABOVE

# Meet Me in Heaven

MEET ME IN HEAVEN, WHEN I LEAVE THIS PLACE
I'LL SEE YOU IN WHEN I'M FULL OF GRACE
I KNOW BEYOND THE GATE, I'LL SEE YOUR FACE
MEET ME IN HEAVEN
THAT'S WHERE I WANT TO GO
BUT FOR NOW I'LL HAVE TO SAY I KNOW
WHEN I AM AM BRIGHT AND FULL OF LIGHT
I KNOW I WILL BE RIGHT BY HIS SIDE
WITH OUR FAITH IN HAND WE'LL BE TOGETHER FOR
ETERNITY
MEET ME IN HEAVEN
MEET ME IN HEAVEN
STEP UP AND TAKE YOUR PLACE
THERE'S ROOM FOR EVERYONE IN HIS PLACE
ALL WE HAVE TO NOW IS LOVE
SO OUR LIGHT CAN REACH HIGH ABOVE MEET ME IN
HEAVEN
MEET ME IN HEAVEN

# To Be Found

DO YOU SEE WHAT IT MEANS
TO BE FOUND
DO YOU KNOW HOW IT FEELS
TO BE LOVED
WHAT NEEDS TO BE SAID
I BELIEVE
WHAT NEEDS TO BE DONE
WHAT HE TELLS ME
LIVING IN HIS WILL
LIVING IN HIS LIGHT
TAKING STEPS TOWARDS HOME
FOLLOW HIS LIGHT I MADE THE CHOICE NOW I WILL
LIVE IT
HAVE FAITH IN YOUR HEART
NEVER GIVE UP
IF YOU SEARCH WITH YOUR HEART
HE WILL BE THERE
YOU HAVE THE STRENGTH
OF THE UNIVERSE
IN YOUR HANDS

# Soul of A Sinner

sinners have souls
just waiting to awaken
sinners have souls
they just need the light to open
i've stayed away so long
because i've been afraid
for who and what i was
but somehow you found me
i couldn't come close
i had a lot of fear
but somehow i got here
didn't take the easy road
didn't come the easy way
but here i am
wanting to stay replace the fear
replace my doubt
so i can feel
your love move through me
baptize my heart
baptize my mind baptize my soul
making me whole
here in the darkness
i found my soul but here in the light
i found my home
that part of me
that is a part of you
i gonna make it
a part of everything i do

sinners have souls
they're just safely tucked away
deep in his arms
waiting to be found
LORD THIS IS THE SOULS OF A SINNER
TALKING TO YOU

# Send Me an Army of Angels

send me an army of angels
send me an army of angels
I have no doubt
they're in the house
to fight the fight with all they're might
send me an army of angels
send me an army of angels
with all they're light
bring down the house
heroes of love
from high above
send me an army of angels
send me an army of angels
to make us strong
to serve the lord
fighting with love
preparing the world
for when he's here
send me an army of angels
send me an army of angels

repeat

# You Don't Know

you don't know where I've been
you don't know what i've done
you don't know what I've seen
the path that I've walked
where i've come from
i've traveled a long way
to get to my home

(CHORUS)
AND NO NO NO I'M NOT GONNA GO
IM STAYING RIGHT HERE
WRAPPED IN HIS LOVE
STAYING RIGHT HERE
WRAPPED IN HIS ARMS AND NO NO NO I WON'T GO

nothing can sway my heart
nothing can sway my mind
i know the truth now
this is where i belong
no no no i'm not going anywhere

(CHORUS)
he opened my heart
and love came in
he opened his arms
and took me in

(CHORUS)
so look at me now
cleansed and new
with his light all around
leading my walk with his love in my heart
leading the way

# Angels From Above

DO THE ANGELS FROM ABOVE
HEAR MY PRAYERS
AM I LOVED
DO I FLY WITH THEM AT NIGHT
WHEN MY SOUL IS IN FLIGHT
DOES MY SOUL GO HOME TO REST
WHEN I RETURN
AM I AT MY BEST
FEELING THEIR LIGHT WITHIN
CLEANSED OF SORROW AND SIN
BECAUSE I FEEL LOVED
AND IN GRACE
I CAN SING THEIR PRAISE
THE ANGELS ARE EVERYWHERE
ALL IT TAKES IS THOUGHT
TO BRING THEM NEAR
WATCHING OVER ALL OF US
NOT HERE FOR JUST ONE OF US
HELPING THE EARTH TO REPAIR
THEY HERE ALL OUR PRAYERS
THEY BRING US BACK
TO LOVE WITH CARE
SHOWING US THE PATH OF LIGHT
WE NEED THE LIGHT
OPEN YOUR HEART
LET THEM IN
THEY OPEN THEIR WINGS
AND COME WITHIN
AND WITH THE LIGHT
THEY GIVE TO YOU

IT MEANT TO SHARE
NOT JUST FOR YOU
LET IT SPREAD WHEREVER YOU GO
AND YOU WILL SEE
A DIFFERENT WORLD
A DIFFERENT WORLD

*Kathleen Santora*

# Im A Little Tired

I'M A LITTLE TIRED LORD
BUT I'M TRYING REALLY HARD
A LITTLE GLAD LORD
JUST KNOWING YOU ARE HERE
JUST DOING MY BEST LORD
TO LIVE IN YOUR WORD
DON'T WANT TO FALL LORD
I KNOW HOW IT FEELS DOWN THERE

I KNOW, I KNOW

IF I LOOK FOR THE LIGHT IN THE DARKNESS
I'LL FIND MY WAY

IF I —-KEEP YOU IN MY HEART
IF I —KEEP YOU IN MY MIND
YOU WILL ALWAYS COME TO BE
BRINGING ME HOME
WITH A SONG IN MY SOUL
KEEPING ME STRONG
TO WHERE I BELONG
NEVER LEAVING YOUR LIGHT
NEVER LEAVING YOUR SIGHT
ALL I NEED TO BE STRONG
IS TO KNOW I BELONG
I KNOW WHEN I CAN HEAR
IT MEANS THAT YOU ARE NEAR
WITH YOUR SONG IN MY HEART

# Come Here

COME HERE LET ME HOLD YOUR HEART
I KNOW YOU ARE ONLY SLEEPING
COME HERE
LET ME HOLD YOUR HEART
I KNOW INSIDE YOU ARE WEEPING
BE STILL IN MY LIGHT
LOOK NO FURTHER FOR LOVE
THAT IS WHERE I EXIST
RETURN YOUR SOUL WITHIN MINE
WHERE ONLY LOVE MATTERS
SEND OUT JUST A THOUGHT
A GENTLE DESIRE
YOUR PERFECT SOUL RESTS WITHIN ME
SAFE FROM ALL HARM
COME AND REST IN REMEMBRANCE
AND YOU WILL FIND HOME
COME HERE
LET ME HOLD YOUR HEART

SING MY PRAISE
AND YOU WILL SEE
A LIGHT SO LOVELY
YOUR EYES WILL SHINE BRIGHTLY
A LOVE SO STRONG
YOUR HEART WILL BEAT IN
RYTHUM OF THE UNIVERSE
SO STRONG AND SWEET
THE LOVE THAT YOU RECEIVE
YOUR DESIRE WILL BE TO SHARE
CONNECTING WITH ALL SOULS
BEARING WITNESS TO MY GRACE

## Message to God

HERE I AM GOD
JUST WAITING FOR THE LIGHT
HERE I AM GOD
JUST TRYING TO FIGHT THE FIGHT
HERE I AM GOD
TRYING TO SEE THE GOOD IN ALL THINGS
NOT LOOKING AT THE BAD
KNOWING ITS NOT RALE
HERE I AM GOD
JUST LOOKING FOR THE TRUTH
THINKING WITH MY HIGHER SELF
GOING DEEP INSIDE
REMEMBERING THE RAY OF LIGHT
WHICH KEEPS ME BY YOUR SIDE
HERE I AM GOD
WANTING MY SPIRIT TO WALK FIRST
BEING ALL YOU WANT ME TO BE
STANDING IN YOUR GRACE
HERE I AM GOD
USE ME AS YOUR MESSENGER
WHILE I AM VISITING THIS PLACE
HERE I AM GOD
LISTENING STILL

# Moment By Moment

MOMENT BY MOMENT
I FEEL THE CHANGE
MOMENT BY MOMENT
I AM NOT THE SAME
MOMENT BY MOMENT
AS I HEAR YOUR VOICE
MOMENT BY MOMENT
AS YOU ENTER MY LIFE
I FEEL THE FREEDOM
THAT YOU GIVE MY MIND
I FEEL THE LOVE
YOU GIVE MY HEART
SENDING ME BLESSINGS
EVERYDAY
SENDING ME GUIDANCE
TO FIND MY WAY
THE LOVE IS SWEET AND PURE
LEAVING NO DOUBT
KNOWING I BELONG
TO THE HEAVENS ABOVE
CHORUS
MOMENT BY MOMENT
I HEAR THE SOUND
YOUR VOICE IS CALLING ME
I KNOW THE SOUND

Printed in the United States
By Bookmasters